Do you know that your thoughts create your feelings, which in turn create what you experience?

Your thoughts are energies, you are energies, the whole universe is energies.

With the energies you send out, you are drawing back to you events that match what you have sent out.

The book you're holding now has actually attracted you, it's exactly what you need right now to move forward in life.

What are your dreams?

Would you like to know how you can create the path to your dreams?

What are your thoughts?

Is there a particular part of your life that needs a push?

This book will help you move forward, it will give you the tips and advice you need.

Read it from page to page or look up a page on feeling only or ask a question and look up a page.

You will always get the answers, advice you need at that moment.

On each page, I have combined a piece of advice from the tarot cards with advice on how to handle the information using the law of attraction.

Then there is also a question linked to the council to further clarify what you need at that particular time.

Finally, there is an affirmation to have with you during the day.

Wishing you all the best with your new conscious life.

You stand firmly with both feet on the ground.

Others look to you as a role model.

You are completely natural and others look up to you.

You give a lot of energy and make people want to be like you and be in your energies.

Be a role model for other people and guide them right.

Give what you want and you will find peace in yourself.

If you want love, give love.

If you want appreciation, give appreciation.

If you want understanding, give understanding.

If you want joy, give joy.

If you want happiness, give happiness.

If you want money, give money.

If you want care, give consideration.

What do I need to give?

I'm safe

Don't be so harsh and reality-obsessed that you get in the way of your own abundance.

Be flexible and playful.

Not everything has to follow rules and protocols.

Bring in some spontaneity and the abundance can come.

Are you in harmony with what you desire?

You're sitting with a pile of unpaid bills that you realize you don't have the money to pay for.

You are sending out a desire for more money.

You keep scrolling through the bills and complaining that you don't have enough money and experience negative emotions such as worry, anger, etc.

You are not in harmony with your desire.

Play, fantasize and dream away. Find the feeling that you are actually where you dream, you are.

Be like a child. The universe can't tell the difference between fantasy and reality, so if you can just feel that you're where you want to be, the universe will take care of the rest.

What spontaneous things can I do?

I'm imaginative

Be patient.

Don't feel hunted.

Don't feel stressed.

You'll get to where you're going when you're going anyway.

There are two kinds of action.

One you force (due to doubts, worries, stress, etc.) by doing something/forcing something to get your wish.

In the second, you let yourself be inspired to achieve your desire.

You see signs, feel that something is going on, act on intuition, only do when it feels good. Allows you to be carried forward without force.

Forcing just feels hard and comes from you becoming impatient, stressed, etc. when you don't see your desire.

Inspired action just feels wonderful because you know that everything will come when it should and that right now you are exactly where you need to be.

How do my actions feel?

I'm patient

Don't rush past life.

It doesn't have to be full speed ahead.

You need to slow down a bit and let life catch up.

Life is not a competition.

Now. At the moment. At this moment. It's the only thing you know something about and can do something with. Know exactly what you have and how you feel. Just right now.

Because what has happened, has already happened and there is nothing you can do about it.

And what happens in a minute, an hour or tomorrow, you can't know anything about, because that's the future.

The only thing you can and must do is look at what you have right now and feel good about it right now.

In this way, you set the tone, the feeling you want for the next minute, hour and day.

And in this way, you can influence what you want in the future without knowing how. Because it's the universe's job to know how, not yours.

Describe the environment I'm in?

I'm enjoying right now

Not everything is black and white.

You feel like you're being treated unfairly or someone is doing something that annoys you.

Try not to judge others but allow others to be who they are.

Let go of the fact that your way is right.

Everyone looks at things differently and comes with different baggage.

You can never feel and think for anyone else.

If you are angry, frustrated or sad about something, it could be an event or a person.

Then you can never blame the person or the event, because it's always your thoughts about this that make you feel the way you do.

What you think, you feel.

So you can never change the situation/person, only your thoughts about it.

So always try to pick out something positive in it or think, aha what am I going to learn from this.

What has upset me today and why?

I am unique

You need to dare.

Challenge yourself a bit to reach and find new ways to your goals/desires.

If you want a change in your life, you have to dare to act on all the signs you get and think in new ways, otherwise life will be exactly the same as it was.

Your inner self always mirrors what you see in your outer world. There are no exceptions.

If you want to see a change in your life, you have to start by changing your inner self and your thoughts.

The most prominent thoughts and feelings you have in your life are those that manifest into the life you are living right now.

Dare to look inward and see what you really feel, only then can you start a change.

What can I do the opposite of what I usually do?

I'm brave

Don't look for happiness outside of you.

Everything you need is within you.

You just need to crack your shell and open up to your true self.

What do you want from the universe?

Is it that nice car, nice furniture, new clothes, mobiles and lots of things you really want.

Or is it that you think all these outward materialistic things make you happy.

Because if you wish for all these things in the hope that you will feel good, you will never get them.

Because the universe responds to your feelings, and if you don't feel good before you get these things, you won't get them either.

You need to make sure you find a way to feel good before you get everything you think you want.

And paradoxically, you won't want all that.

But happiness is always within you and not in the outward materialistic.

Start by being grateful with what you have.

What makes me feel good?

I'm grateful

Sometimes you have to step over and out of your own values.

Don't mess them up and splash them on others.

You need to see things from other perspectives as well.

You see and perceive the world, things, events and people, etc., in your own way. This depends on how you have grown up, experiences in life, what you believe in, your values and what you have been taught.

And so does everyone else.

And that's ok.

It's when you think others should behave, behave in a certain way that fits your world that things go wrong. You get frustrated, angry, or sad. And automatically attracts you more of it.

Allow others to have their world and let it be ok. Stop having expectations of how things should be, let it be as it is.

What are my values?

I'm permissive

You let the old chase you.

You are a slave to your own whip.

You need to try to see more clearly who you really are and who you think you are because of the baggage you have with you.

Time to lighten the backpack a bit.

Is this natural for me? Feel inwards, does it make you feel good? Well, then it's natural for you.

Is it natural for me to do this? Does it feel good? Well, then it's natural for you.

Don't think normally in situations. That this is how we have normally done when I grew up, this is how normal is to feel, this is how you normally do not, things like that can not normally happen.

There is no Normal.

The only thing that exists and should exist is: Is this natural for me? Does this feel natural to me?

What can I let go of that isn't really mine?

I'm natural

You feel a sadness.

A loneliness.

Hard to find the joy.

The world feels heavy and grey.

You own your thoughts and it is they who create the feelings in you which in turn attracts similar thoughts/feelings through what you experience in life.

If you feel sadness, you attract more of sadness.

If you feel lonely, you get more of it.

If you feel worried, you will be more worried.

What you need to do is find your joy in the little things. Start by identifying what thoughts are making you sad and turn it around. See how you want it instead.

I want to be happy

I want company

I want to be calm

Ok what makes me happy then?

Does eating a crispbread sandwich, watching funny clips on youtube, watching your cats play, hugging your child, riding a bike, etc.

Then do it as often as you can to raise your thoughts to a feel good state, because then the Law of Attraction automatically sends you more things to feel good about.

What can I turn around for thought today?

I choose joy

Just because you get things doesn't mean others don't.

You think that if you give to some, you will turn your back on others.

If you want things for yourself, someone else will be left without.

You came into this world to live in abundance. But over the course of your life, you've lost it because society, family, and friends have imprinted you with limiting thoughts.

There will never be an end in the universe, there is more than enough for everyone.

Just because you want a red car doesn't mean that everyone else who also wants a red car won't get it. And by the way, not everyone else wants a red car. Someone wants a blue, green, or yellow.

Nothing is too big or too much universe.

It's only your own limiting thoughts about what's too big that stops you.

For the universe, $100,000 is not harder than $1, it's you who thinks it's harder.

If you think that it is not for everyone, you have a lack mindset and it is not positive thoughts, because then you will have more deficiency.

Trust that there is what everyone should have.

What is my limiting thought right now?

I am worthy of everything

Dream about your goals and desires.

See the treasure chest at the end of the rainbow.

Believe in yourself and your inner nakedness.

Fantasize more.

If we want to achieve our dreams and change the direction of our lives, we have to learn new things and walk new paths.

Feel within, trust your intuition, and see all the signs around us.

Open your senses and pay attention to your surroundings.

You may see an ad that says something that reminds you of what you want, sees something written somewhere, often you hear someone say something similar, hear a song about it or just get an inspiration to do something.

Then you should know that it is the universe telling you that it is coming and the inspiration tells you that now is the best time to act to continue towards your wish.

So trust yourself and your gut.

What can I open myself up to today?

I'm open to signs

Climb on, you'll soon be up.

You'll see a solution to everything.

The tide is turning.

You start to see opportunities instead of problems.

You see that you have something to learn from everything.

Sometimes it can seem like you've done everything right and yet you think that it goes wrong when it finally comes true or that it doesn't turn out the way you want it to.

But then you have to rest in the feeling that it wasn't meant to be for you anyway and that something else much better is going on in the future that you can't see right now. But trust that the universe always has your best interests as the number one priority.

It's just a matter of moving forward.

If you look back at different events in your life, I can almost guarantee that you will find a meaning in all the so-called defeats.

So see all the little setbacks as life lessons.

Everything has a meaning in life.

In which area do I often see problems?

I see opportunities

The feeling of jealousy, jealousy is there right now.

Feels unfair because others have what I want.

I'm going to fight for what I'm going to have.

Always having to struggle with everything and everyone else seems to go on a shrimp sandwich through life.

What do you need to do then?

You have to rejoice with them, be in their feeling and know that everything is there for you too as long as you can let go of jealousy and rejoice with others.

Try to put yourself in their shoes and the universe will respond right away by giving you experiences that match those feelings as well.

There's enough for you and the universe supports you.

If you see someone who has won a lot of money, feel their joy.

If you see a couple newly in love, feel their joy and happiness, be infected by it. Imagine how wonderful it is to have that tingling feeling in your stomach and those twinkling eyes.

Be happy for others.

Who can I rejoice with today?
I'm compassionate

Anything is possible.

You just have to dare to throw yourself down and dare to do/think new.

Follow the winds of change and pave a new path for yourself.

What values do you bring with you in life?

What have you been told all your life?

What has marked you?

The fact is that we get a lot of "truths" about things during our upbringing.

Parents, friends, and society say things that we believe in and take as truths about both ourselves and the world.

What do you bring with you?

Life is a struggle! No, it's not, only if you think so.

Work hard for your money! No, not at all, you are worthy of abundance by just being you.

Money doesn't grow on trees! Oh yes, only you can believe it.

Real love doesn't exist! Oh yes and it's there for you.

Happiness is for everyone else! No, it's within you. You just need to listen to yourself more and impress yourself with your own new truths.

What "truths" do you have with you?

I'm coming along

You are the creator of your own future.

You sit at the loom and decide which threads and colors the tablecloth should have.

The color you put in is the color that comes out at the front.

I can never blame you and say that I didn't want that color there, when you're the one who wove it in.

To change your reality, you have to change yourself and your feelings.

You have attracted everything that you have in your life right now with your thoughts that have evoked certain emotions that the universe is responding to.

If there is a lot and strong emotions involved, it will come faster.

So your happiness and joy depend entirely on you.

Most people think about what they *don't* want. But the law of attraction doesn't care that you *don't* want what you're thinking about, it responds to your feelings that you have for what you're thinking about.

Don't *think* about sausages!

I bet that's exactly what you did.

Do you understand..

Your brain didn't register the word *not,* but only on what you were thinking of, falukorv. So it is with the universe.

Think about what you want instead.

What do I have strong feelings about?

I get what I want

The confusion is total.

Which way should I go, how should I do, what should I do.

There are so many choices in life.

What do I want?

How do I want my life?

What do I want to do?

What do I want out of life?

What's missing?

Sometimes you get confused and don't really know what you want or if you're on the right track.

Sit down and write a list of your expectations in life.

You don't get what you want, but what you expect.

Go through and clarify every area of your life, job, money, relationships, health, etc.

Write down how you want it to be in each area, what you expect.

Be very clear and detailed without thinking about all possible obstacles, write what you want.

Because the universe has a great sense of humor too, you know.

Tired and not wanting to get up so early in the morning, can result in 1.5 hours of oversleeping.

Writing it down also makes it more powerful, so it's a recommendation to get into the habit of writing down what you want.

What do I want?

I'm clear

Do you feel like you've lost a piece of your life puzzle?

Something is missing in your life.

Maybe this book can help you put the last bit together.

But at the same time, the puzzle of life is never finished. You grow and change all the time.

All the pieces may not need to be in place right away.

The important thing is to see the big picture. Maybe it works just as well without that last piece of the puzzle, for a while anyway.

When we temporarily lose some part of our life puzzle, then we tend to put all our focus on the missing piece of the puzzle.

We get sad, worried, angry, etc. because we don't have that piece of the puzzle.

What we then do is attract more of those feelings, which can result in us losing more pieces of the puzzle.

Don't let all your happiness and well-being depend on a single piece of the puzzle. Make sure to have a good balance and above all see all the pieces you have left and be grateful and happy with that.

You survive if a piece of love has disappeared temporarily. Think about all the parts you have left instead and have faith that the universe will deliver a new piece when you are ready.

Which piece of the puzzle am I okay without?

I see the big picture

You feel guilty, shame about something.

It chases you and you have a hard time letting go of it.

Feels threatening and you feel haunted by it.

You never feel free.

Feeling guilty and ashamed about something prevents you from progressing and going against your desires. It's holding you back, and it's only in your thoughts.

It's connected to something that has happened. And it's already over, you can never change what has already happened and therefore the guilt is only in your thoughts.

What has happened is already over, past, finito, and over. So then the event that created the debt is also over and you can't possibly change it, so why feel guilty.

The only reality you have is right now and *right now* you are free and you have nothing to feel guilty about.

Let the past be past and the future is the future and you don't know anything about it right now.

Let go of the thought debt now. Now it's a new day and now you know things you didn't do yesterday.

What can I let go of for guilt?

I'm free

I'm standing a bit still now.

Pretty uneventful, you feel.

Standing in the same place and just waiting.

New winds need to come.

It can be good to land from time to time. Even if it feels like nothing is happening, things are happening all the time.

It doesn't have to be visible in physical form or things, there's a lot going on inside.

It is the universe's way of telling us that now is the time to stop and not chase the outward visible, but now is the time for spiritual work.

What do I really want to be, how do I really want to be. The soul needs to catch up. If you're too focused on the exterior, it feels like it's at a complete standstill now.

Start meditating, start doing yoga and long walks, and you'll find a whole new approach to yourself and the world.

Know that you are always exactly where you should be and listen inward from time to time.

How can I calm down today?

I'm calm

Carry your heart with ease.

Trust your feelings and be true to yourself.

The heart, intuition and gut feeling are what is true and will always lead you in the right direction.

Life usually moves at breakneck speed and there is little time for reflection. Decisions can often be wrong and you can regret things.

When you are faced with a decision or a choice of any kind and don't know what to do.

Then you can consult your inner self. Consult your heart, intuition, and gut feeling.

Sit still and ask the question and feel how it feels. If it feels good in your stomach, then you should do it, but if you get an uncomfortable feeling, your inner advice is to abstain.

You feel this quite easily actually as long as you take the time for the few minutes it takes. You will always get an answer and the more you practice this, the clearer it becomes.

What can I consult today?

I trust my gut

Now things are happening.

You've set the ball in motion.

You've been actively doing something to get closer to your desire.

If you didn't think it was impossible (your dream, it, what you want) what would you do?

What steps would you take towards your dream?

Do it, just as you would if the dream were here right now. Take the plunge and move towards your dreams. You don't have to see all the way, you just need to take the first step.

The universe will do everything it can to help you move forward, making sure that people, circumstances and events come your way and lead you on.

What step can I take today?

I can act

There's a lot of stress right now.

I feel like time is running out.

You just wander around and wait and beg hurry, hurry.

Sometimes you want something so much and get too focused on the outcome of the desire that it creates insecurity, fears, doubts and despair.

I don't have it yet! Hurry, hurry.

Then the focus shifts to what you don't have and it won't.

You have to have patience and trust that the universe always delivers when you let it go and just get on with your life.

You have to feel that life is ok anyway, even if you don't get what you desire. And if you get what you want, that's an added bonus.

Say: I've managed my whole life without this, so I'm sure I'll be able to do it in the future as well. It's just something I want, but don't need for my well-being.

What am I stressed about?

I'm ok

Now you are reaping what you sowed before.

As you sow, you will reap.

Now and onwards, you will have the life you created yesterday.

All thoughts/feelings are seeds.

What's important is that you stop seeing yourself as a victim of circumstances.

Well, that and I didn't want that.

Well, I didn't want to experience that.

Well, it wasn't my fault.

Well, it did this and that.

Well, you've attracted all that. Maybe not the specific event, but the event *always* matches your innermost feeling and mood. And the universe always delivers a match using circumstances and situations to you, anything else is impossible.

If you think about a bad situation in your life and be honest now about how you really felt about your innermost feelings at the time, I guarantee that it matches.

So stop making yourself a victim.

Look at yourself how you feel, what energies you think, feel and send out.

Then you know what's coming.

What seeds have I sown?

I am a creator

Standing safe and stable now.

You've come to a point where it might be time to start looking around and letting other people in.

You don't have to put walls around you and protect yourself.

Dare to look around and discover new things.

When you put up protection around yourself, you do it out of different fears you have.

And then you continue to attract circumstances that allow you to retain your fears.

At some point you have to let go if you want a change in your life.

Start looking around for new opportunities and start trusting that there is something bigger than you that wants the best for you and supports you.

Trust yourself, love yourself for who you are because you are perfect just because you exist.

If you can't love yourself, you have no love to give others either. You can't possibly give something you don't have yourself.

Who can I let in today?

I dare

Great events are coming.

A lot of changes are going on.

Can feel like you're being swept away towards something dangerous and unknown.

When you consciously start working with the law of attraction and yourself, a lot of unknown feelings can emerge in you.

Things you didn't even know about yourself may come up.

You may even feel worse for a while and feel like you're drowning.

But see it as something positive and that you have to go through in order to move forward.

Without processing the old, it will remain in you and hinder your path forward towards your dreams.

So let it be a little turbulent from time to time and know that after rain comes sunshine. And that the purge is something positive to take you further.

Have any new feelings surfaced in me?

I can be myself

Let life sprout naturally.

Everything you need is there for you naturally.

You are nourished by nature.

You are nourished by pure love.

You are nourished by the entire universe.

Feel that you are one with everything, everything is connected.

Try to be in as natural a shape as possible. You came into this world effortlessly and you are meant to continue your life's journey in the same spirit.

Think about when you were in your mother's womb for the first nine months and developed without any effort and mixture of yourself. You evolved quite naturally and trusted that you would get the nose, foot, heart, etc. that you would have. You didn't question all the time, where's my nose? Will it? And when? You had complete trust in nature to provide you with what you needed.

Keep going and trust the natural flow and that you get what you should have in life without effort.

What do I know that will always work out?

I'm in the flow

Stubbornness and struggle are in focus now.

There are conflicts around you that you are easily drawn into.

Can be with outsiders, but also with yourself.

Instead of explaining yourself and defending yourself in something, just let it be. Don't get caught up in the opposites right or wrong.

Don't feel the necessity of being right, because then you'll put yourself above others and tell them they're wrong. And who really decides what is right or wrong?

You perceive things in your own way depending on your upbringing, experiences, etc.

And so does everyone else. And that's ok.

It's when you think others should behave, behave in a certain way that fits your world that things go wrong. Then there will be conflicts, you will be frustrated, angry or sad.

So allow others to have their world and let it be ok.

Am I in any conflict right now?

I'm humbled

Believe that you are lucky.

Believe that you will succeed.

Open your fortune cookie and have faith.

Have faith.

There are so many people who feel bad, unlucky, are unhappy and don't have this or that.

And yet we have so much to be thankful for.

A roof over our heads, running water, toilet, often a car, food, clothes to put on when it gets cold, some kind of family, etc

And yet we only see how unhappy we are.

Now I sound a bit harsh maybe, but if you only expect shit, you only get shit.

Then it doesn't matter how much you wish for something else.

Start expecting luck too, you can succeed in anything you want.

It's with you.

In which areas do I usually get lucky?

I'm lucky

Enjoy life. Pamper yourself.

Get out there and sit down and enjoy just being a part of this universe.

Love yourself.

Focus on your positive qualities, and even more wonderful qualities will come out of you.

Treat yourself the way you treat your best friend.

Stop trying to fit in to feel a sense of community, you are hiding yourself and who you really are then.

You are an asset to humanity because you are unique and your qualities make you invaluable in the world. Everyone needs for the balance of the universe.

What advice would I give my best friend now?

I'm my best friend

Sees life as a tug-of-war.

Have to fight most of the time.

Stubbornness can get in the way and can hurt others.

Let go and see all the beauty around you and all the warmth that exists.

Are you one of those who are of the opinion that you have to work hard for what you want and that life is constantly a struggle to get what you want.

And you struggle and struggle but never seem to get what you want anyway.

Then I now say Congratulations, you have now proven to yourself all your life so far that that mindset obviously does not work.

Now it's time for a new path, stop struggling.

Don't do anything, don't strive for more, let go of the addiction to things and give up.

What have I always struggled with?

I can let go

Continue on your dream/vision.

See the result in front of you.

You're building something big and sustainable now.

Make sure to focus on your dream now and see the end result. It's not your job to figure out the When, Where, and How of your vision. Your job is to see the finished result.

Many of history's inventors and builders didn't know how to go about it, but they clearly saw the result they wanted.

It is the job of the universe to bring to you paths, circumstances, and people that benefit your dream.

You don't have the capacity to figure out how while the universe has unlimited resources to provide you.

If you start interfering, you stop the natural flow to you.

What is my dream?

I'm focused

Don't think about it anymore, set off on your life's journey.

Take active steps towards your dream.

Don't wait any longer.

Don't hesitate any longer.

Often because you don't know how to do it, how to do it or it feels overwhelming and you don't know where to start, a dream remains just a dream or wish.

Stop thinking so big, you don't have to see all the way.

If you're going from Luleå to Kalmar, you can't stop going just because you can't see all the way, right?

You trust that the road will show itself with the help of various signs such as gps.

You just start the journey by driving away.

So it is with your dreams too, you just need to start and the rest will appear.

What's holding me back?

I trust that my path will show itself

Make peace with everyone and everything.

Embrace all differences.

Think of it as an opportunity.

Take everyone by the hand and exclude no one.

When you are in harmony with yourself, you feel secure and happy with who you are and what you have.

Then you also allow others to be who they are.

Then you don't have the need to correct someone, criticize someone, be right or wrong about something. Then you just let others be who they are.

It's all the differences in this world that create contrasts so we can see what we want.

What makes me unique?

I love differences

You have the power over your life and no one else.

Don't leave your life and well-being to others.

Be a conductor and direct your own life.

Being angry, frustrated, annoyed and hating someone else only affects yourself.

You're the one walking around with those feelings.

The person in question doesn't know those feelings.

It's like drinking poison and hoping the other person will die.

So let others be who they are and don't walk around with a lot of unhealthy feelings because then they control your life.

Because you attract what you feel.

Don't let them affect you.

What do I blame on others?

I'm in charge of my life

You're sitting very still now and just waiting.

What are you waiting for?

You can't see how long something will take if you don't do something inspiring yourself.

Don't wait for life to happen.

Don't wait for it to turn around.

Don't wait for this and that.

Don't wait for anyone.

Don't wait for if I had.

Don't wait for when.

Don't wait.

Then you will have to wait for the rest of your life. Is that the way you want your life, an eternal wait for something to happen. Because if you walk around with the feeling that you are waiting for a lot of things to happen, then the law of attraction makes sure that you get eternal waiting.

You make life happen.

You turn your life around.

You make it so and that comes.

You make someone come.

You make it happen.

You do.

What am I waiting for to happen?
I inspire

Don't let life become a tug-of-war between you and the universe.

Let the universe deliver what you're supposed to have.

Try not to pull and steer it.

How long it takes to get something depends entirely on you.

The more you can let go and trust the universe, the faster it goes.

It's only your own limitations on what's possible and what's not that stops the flow to you.

And when you start to interfere, try to decide how something should be done and pull in some direction.

What are my limiting thoughts?

I trust the universe

Now is the time for you to become the judge of your own life.

You can't continue to live your life according to how others have judged, thought and felt about you.

Take the helm.

It's really important that you let the past be the past, because now is now.

Don't let old things from the past hang with you today so you feel bad about them.

Don't let anyone else put a label on you about what and how you are.

Don't let that stop you.

Don't let it punish you.

Don't punish yourself for past sins. Because you did the best you could with the knowledge you had at the time.

Now it's new, now you know something else, now you have new knowledge and experience.

You're not the same person you were 5, 10, 15 or 20 years ago, so stop and let it define and judge you.

What do others say about me now?

I'm happy with myself

The calm comes and you feel very satisfied right now.

Looking ahead with curiosity, playfulness and anticipation.

Look at your life with outside eyes sometimes.

You'll be sure to see that it's probably not that bad after all.

Most likely, you have more than enough things, you probably have food, you have a roof over your head, etc

But still, you strive for more. Why?

Our materialistic society often incites us to consume more and more.

Get out of that rush and be happy with what you have, rather get rid of things and you will be free in your soul. Don't let any things own you.

What kind of things do I have that owns me?

I'm having a very good time

You have an addiction that you want to get rid of.

Addiction controls you.

You have a hard time coming down to earth and being yourself because of this because it controls you and not the other way around.

To say that quitting an addiction is hard to get rid of is just fooling yourself.

What's hard is to keep the dependency. It's much more difficult to be addicted to something than not to be one.

Take smoking, for example.

You must always make sure to have cigarettes.

You always have to have money, you have to go to the store and buy cigarettes, you have to open the package, you always have to make sure you have a lighter with you, you always have to make sure you have time to smoke and you have to look for places where you can smoke, etc.

It's much easier not to do it because then you don't have to do anything more than not do it.

What kind of addiction do I have?

I'm honest

Love is in your life as long as you allow it.

You've been hit by Cupid's arrows and you can shoot love arrows yourself now.

Life doesn't repeat, so why go and keep on saving all the love that you have inside you.

Feel love for yourself and others and it will give you back a thousandfold.

Spread the love around you and see, feel the joy of the recipients.

You will be happy, happy and full of love if someone else gives you love.

Give unconditional love, you can never go wrong. Love can never end.

It dissolves stress, hatred, worry, sadness, etc.

Who can I shower with love today?

I am loving

Stand up for yourself.

Be your own best friend.

You have to trust yourself and see yourself as worthy of all the good things in this world.

Take care of yourself, support yourself and make yourself feel good.

Be a little ego. You have to be able to love yourself before you can give love to others. You have to consider yourself worth everything and that you have a lot of value. Otherwise, the universe can't send you everything you're worth.

Do exactly what you would do for your best friend.

What does your friend (you) need to hear today?

That she is wise, beautiful, generous, kind, caring, has beautiful eyes, wonderful humor, encouraging, spreads joy, etc

You are all this and more. Embrace it and be your own best friend.

What can I do for myself today?

I'm caring

Look up and look around.

Be curious and learn from others.

Look at all the people who come into your life as your own private teachers.

Everyone comes with different messages.

Some trait that you also want or something you don't want shows you the person.

Identify what and you grow as a person.

Who can I learn from today?

I'm curious

You are exposed to a wealth of information, assessment, decisions and values on a daily basis.

Remember that it is always your choice in any situation how you will choose to take things. Whether you choose consciously or unconsciously.

And all the choices you've made so far affect everything that's happening right now.

If we are to be able to sow what we harvest, we need to make conscious choices.

The unconscious choices we make automatically because of how we have been learned with different things throughout life. How we repeat our reactions to different situations.

Start becoming aware of your reactions and the choices you make, and you can actively start choosing.

What choices do I make today?

I live consciously

Surprises await you.

Someone wants to come into your life.

Are you ready to open the door.

Do you allow all the glorious things to come to you or do you resist it?

When you allow it, you just go with life without trying to control it.

You let go of all worries about everything and have full trust.

You talk about what you want and experience instead of talking about what you don't have and don't want to experience.

You think, feel, act as if you already have what you want.

You are grateful for what you have.

You're happy with what you have and see everything else as a bonus.

What words do I use when I speak?

I'm attentive

You're looking for your key.

You try things out because you know there's something more to life.

You want life to be about something more.

Do you have any questions about whether life should just be like this? Is it nothing more? What's the point, anyway? Is this life?

You don't quite get the hang of it, but still, you know it should be something more.

Then it's time to think about what kind of life philosophy/beliefs/basic values you want.

Everyone needs something like that to follow. A belief in something more that can be a guide.

Look back a little and see if you can find a common thread in your interests, what has always appealed to you. What you've read a lot about, looked at a lot and what you've wanted to know more about. Then you get some clues about what your philosophy might be and look further from there.

Can I see a common thread in my life?

I'm investigative

You can't really relax and enjoy your successes.

You think somewhere that you still have to suffer and fight.

You've come a long way and achieved the success you've dreamed of.

But don't consider yourself worthy.

Once you get the money.

When you feel joy and happiness in life.

Enjoy it and know it's exactly how it should be.

You are worth it and everything has a meaning.

Many who win, for example, large sums of money are still in their old values, poor thinking and not being worth it.

And all of a sudden, they're poor again because of it. Because the universe has to deliver so that it matches your innermost being. And feeling poor doesn't match having a lot of money.

So gratefully accept what you get, whatever it is, it is not handed out by chance.

You should have it right now, maybe to be able to help someone else.

Maybe for yourself.

But whatever it is, enjoy and be grateful.

How do I enjoy what I get?

Everything that comes to me is meant to

The password to the universe.

The password to joy.

The password to happiness.

The password to the dreams.

The password to the Law of Attraction.

The password is Gratitude.

If you can't feel gratitude for what you have right now, you can't possibly attract things to be grateful for.

If you can't feel gratitude for what you have now, you have a sense of lack, dissatisfaction and loss within you.

And that's not a good feeling to walk around with.

There is a little word that brings joy, happiness, and peace. It cleans up all the negativity in your life and changes you in a positive direction.

Thanks

What am I thankful for today?

Thank you for everything in my life

Now is the time to say goodbye to all the old baggage and gain new experiences.

Let go of everything with pride.

Let go of your addiction to things or you won't get what you desire.

You should keep the intention to get what you want, but let go of your dependence on the outcome.

Everything here in the physical world is symbols, cars, houses, banknotes, clothes, etc. and they come and go.

The addiction comes from the fact that it is always symbols you think you need. Then we become prisoners of helplessness, hopelessness, worldly things and trifles.

We think that everything will work out and be fine as long as we get these symbols, but just like I mentioned, these are fleeting and you will be on the hunt for life.

Say goodbye to the old way of thinking and step into the unknown where you can start being creative.

What do I think will make me feel better?

I can let things go

Let go of your addiction to money.

Money is not the only source of abundance.

Step up and see all the other possibilities.

Do you think it's only money that can give you what you want?

If I just get so and so much, I can do it.

What do you want to do? What do you want? What do you want to buy?

Let go of the focus on the fact that you need to have money first.

See the thing you want, feel like you have it already.

The universe has endless ways to give you what you want without the involvement of money.

See the end goal instead, what you would like to have.

For example, if you want a new TV but don't consider yourself to have the money, don't see the money you need, but see yourself with a TV.

You can get it as a gift, you can win a contest, you can get it at a huge sale price, etc.

So let go of the money focus and focus on what you

want.

Am I locked into money?
* I focus on feeling good*

You're about to go into a little dip.

An event has triggered this.

Try to look at this from the outside and as an isolated incident. It's just a small thing in your life.

If you step out of your lifeline, you can see more clearly that this is just a short period of your entire life.

A bit like when you have an infant with colic, when you're in it it's hell, but afterwards you can see that it was only maybe 3 months of my whole life in maybe 80 years.

Know that it won't last forever and let go of control and let yourself feel the way you do, but work your way on to get back up. And have faith that you'll get back up because you've done that before.

Can I see which event triggered this?

* I'm strong*

Fix what needs to be repaired in order for you to be able to move forward.

But do it for your own sake and not for the ego's sake.

Achievement, appraisal, and the approval of others, that's what your ego seeks.

Do things for your own sake and because it feels good inside you, completely independent of whether you are going to perform something, be valued or get someone's approval.

It shouldn't matter.

The most important thing is that you get pleasure from it, that you contribute something, that you can help someone. The ego is not who you are, but it is your social mask that thrives on being liked by others and is a role you play.

Be yourself soul and love yourself for what you do.

What has my ego been seeking today?

* I am myself*

In today's stressful society with all the demands that exist, it is important that you find balance and calm in something.

In order for you to feel as good as possible, it is important that you find balance in your life. That you find a way for you to unwind and sort all the impressions you get.

We need to be in stillness for a little while every day for our own reflection. Quiet your thoughts. Quiet your mind. Charge your batteries.

This is different for each person, but meditation is a recommendation.

Sit in silence and just breathe for a quarter of an hour a day, let the thoughts come and go completely naturally without getting stuck in them. Just let them go. Can be easier if you count from 1-10 and then start over again and focus on the count. It can be hard at first but it's getting easier and easier so don't give up and don't be too yourself.

When is the best time for me to be in stillness?

I breathe deeply

Believe in yourself.

If you think something, stand by it.

You are unique and contribute to this world with your own wisdom.

Don't be afraid to express your needs, but don't expect everyone to think alike.

Everyone has their own free will and it should be that way.

It's when you think others should think like you that you feel bad.

Also practice not always expressing what you think, you don't have to be right or wrong.

It's a judgmental mindset and what you judge reflects back on you.

If you do, take the opportunity to see what you can learn about yourself to become freer.

Do I have a situation where I'm quick to judge?

* I am unique*

Love is the greatest.

Both to yourself and others.

Love can alleviate everything.

Greatest of all is love. Feel love for everything. Give love unconditionally.

Remember that what you give, you get back. Don't skimp on love because there is no end, love can never end.

You can dissolve everything with love. Send love to everyone, even your so-called enemies.

Holding a grudge against someone only backfires on you. Pour love thoughts into everything.

You will feel the knots dissolve. Everyone deserves love by just being, including you. There should be no conditions set on who will receive love.

Can I give a little extra love to someone today?

* I spread love*

Dare to step out of the box.

If you stay in the same routines, you will have the same life.

Often we do things on a routine basis. We do our chores in the same order every single day. We do what we usually do.

If we are going to do laundry, clean and shop during a day, we almost always do it in a certain order. For example, always start with the laundry, then cleaning and end with shopping. We just do this on a routine basis, whether we want to or feel like it.

Start by feeling first thing in the morning to see which one it would feel best to start with. This will put you in a better flow throughout the day. You step out of the box and listen to your inner self that is always there to guide you to your best.

What are my routines?

I'm thinking new

Now life is playing.

You see all the beauty that exists in the world.

Enjoy and make the most of it.

You feel playful and adventurous.

When you have flow in life, nothing feels impossible. Save all the memories like a photo bank in your head, but above all, save the feeling you have. Then you can think about that memory when you don't have this flow, because life goes a bit up and down, but then you can pick up this image and the feeling you have for it and you lift yourself up much faster.

Because as we all know, your brain doesn't know if it's something real or imaginary you're feeling, so as long as you can conjure up the feeling you want in life, the universe has to deliver matching events.

What wonderful memories do I have to pick up?

* I'm looking for wonderful feelings*

You're on the right track.

But sometimes it feels like you're floating on a slack line.

Make sure to just stay focused where you're going and the rest will take care of itself.

You have many choices in life and you can change your mind along the way to the goal.

What I know today, I won't have to hold on to in two days. I may have received new information that gives me a new path towards my goal.

Have the courage to change.

As long as you are focused on your dream and goals, the universe will guide you in the right direction, even if it means changing plans. The universe always has a plan with its changes, all for your good.

What do I stubbornly hold on to?

I'm on the right track

You begin to suspect that there is some great force at work for you.

Is it coincidence, luck or is there some force in the universe.

You find yourself in circumstances that may not be just coincidence.

Everyone thinks I need some kind of guidance in life. Some philosophy of life to follow. That we have some basic value in life.

Be curious and find out more about things that come to you, even if you just think it's a coincidence. It's a force that tries to show you the way. Give it a go and be more open-minded.

If texts, music, books and TV shows start to appear about something special, it's the universe that wants to call your attention to find your way.

We feel so much better when we have found our purpose in life and you have someone who watches over you, wants to help you if you just allow that opportunity.

Do I see something very often?

* I'm protected*

Anything you want, you can have.

Anything is possible.

Nothing is impossible for the universe.

See the universe as Alladin, he says, your desire is my law.

And so it is, what you can see and feel, you can get.

It's just for you to wish and relax.

Think of the universe as a mail-order catalogue, you tell us what you want, order and then you let it go and trust that it will come.

It's exactly the same as your wishes, tell them what you want in life and send out an order and then it's a matter of letting it go and trusting delivery.

When you order a pair of pants, you don't start hesitating, think about if they will come and when they will arrive and how they will come, you trust that they will come.

What do I wish for today?

I'm a magnet

Victory.

You've climbed up and gotten over your limiting thoughts about money.

Often it's not your own limitations that hold you back, but it's other people's limitations that you've taken to heart during your upbringing.

Ask yourself: What did you hear about money growing up? Was there money? Was there a shortage? Was it saved or wasted? Was it joy around money or just arguments?

What were your experiences with money growing up?

All of this has influenced you to believe a lot of things about money, which may not be true at all today.

Think about it and question if it really is like that or if it can be in another way and turn it into something positive.

Can I find my limitations?

* I'm here and now*

Male and female.

Black or white.

Sadness or joy.

It's very either or in your life right now.

Does it really need to be one or the other.

There are always two polar opposites to each other. But that's just so that we can see more clearly what we want and not to judge by.

You see something long, just because there are cards too. But one does not exclude the other and neither is more right or wrong than the other.

See everything for what it is without judging. See everything for where it is without having to be right or wrong.

Can I be a spectator today?

I'm free

You're facing a big and tough decision now.

You have two possibilities here.

It's solving it or being defeated by it.

Try to see yourself from a different angle, lift yourself out of yourself, so to speak, and look at the problem from the outside.

The saying that you always see solutions to other people's problems is very true.

Because how many times have you not seen clearly what someone else should do, but not what you need to do yourself.

Step out of yourself and put the problem into perspective. If this applied to someone else, what would your advice be.

Give advice to yourself. Can be difficult when you're in the middle of it, but try to be a third party here.

And above all, follow your own advice, you know deep down what is right.

What advice do I have for myself today?

I'm my best friend

What you sow, you will reap.

You are very blooming right now and can see all the big beautiful flowers you have sown.

You feel good and reap good things.

Now you see that all the work you've put into yourself is having an effect.

You see that you have to feel good first in your mind, in order for everything good to come in reality.

"I believe it when I see it" is what many people say and think.

You need to turn it around and say, "You'll see it, when you believe it."

You have to start believing that you have what you want already.

You have to see that it's possible before you see it. Feel with your whole self that it is there. Do everything you can to feel it. Surround yourself with the people who have what you want, look at what you want, buy little things that make you feel the way you want.

A lot of things exist even though we can't see them. If you only believe what you see, then why are you paying the electricity bill? You don't see the electricity and yet you know it's there.

What do I want to see before I believe it?

Today I'm thinking the opposite

Even if you're different from everyone else, you feel safe with it.

You know your worth and that you matter.

Walking straight in the back and following your path.

You should know that you are here on earth for one reason and that is to add your uniqueness.

You are a totally unique creation and there is no one else like you.

Therefore, you need to stop living and try to be like everyone else. You shouldn't be like everyone else, you shouldn't live like others, do like others.

You have to create your own unique path through life, that's your job.

You should be true to yourself and realize that you are an asset just the way you are and without changing anything to fit in.

What makes me me?

I am an asset to the world

Pleasure is one of your great passions.

You love the freedom of nature and just being.

Soak up the energies of nature.

Look around in nature. Look at all the beauty that is around you.

It's yours to enjoy. Nature offers a magnificence without the slightest effort.

Look at how everything thrives and grows. Completely natural. Be like nature and grow naturally without putting in that much effort. Go with your natural flow.

The water doesn't ask anything back to irrigate the flowers. The sun asks nothing in return to provide warmth and energy to nature. They just do what they're there for.

So do you.

When do I feel most natural?

I'm natural

There are concerns. You need answers to something you're thinking about.

You need help with something but may feel a little left out then.

Sometimes you are faced with different issues. At crossroads in life. Both positive and negative.

Ask the question to the universe and wait for an answer. Because you will get answers. Can come in many different ways, for example someone who says something, there is a person in your life with answers, you read something, etc.

Now it's up to you to use your intuition and see the answers as answers. And dare to follow them.

Don't worry you'll miss out, because the universe doesn't give up. It may just take a little longer and be a more tedious path to your answer, but you will always get an answer. And you'll learn a lot along the way.

If you see the signs right away and know how to shop on them, it will go faster and straighter where you want to go.

What am I looking for?

I'm actively seeking answers today

What you're doing now.

Or what you think you'd like.

That is absolutely right.

Trust yourself all the time, if it's right, it's easy and if it's easy, it's right, it's as simple as that.

When you get one of those flashing ideas, that kind of just comes as a bolt from the blue, a whim.

Then it's the right thing to do and you should act on that whim immediately. Because it is the universe telling you that now is the right time to do what you have in mind, there is no more right time than right now.

And if you act then, even more will fall into place and you will have whims all the time that will lead you exactly where you are going.

So your task is to follow your whims and the universe will guide you further.

What does the universe want me to act on?

Today I follow my whims

You have so much to be thankful for right now.

You feel very satisfied with life and can take everything in your stride.

You can really relax knowing that everything is exactly as it should be.

Feeling gratitude is probably the most important thing you can do. It's the most important thing in your life and it's the most important thing in this book.

If you can't feel gratitude for what you have, you'll never get anything better.

If you don't feel gratitude, you have a feeling of lack in you, a loss, an emptiness and you can only get it back.

Get into the habit of writing ten things a day that you are grateful for and you will see that your life will change in a positive direction.

Everyone has something to be thankful for.

Water in the tap, clothes on the body, food, a bed, a toilet, a coffee cup, pets, nature, etc.

Start writing and thoughts of what you have to be thankful for will come to you more and more.

What do I have to be thankful for?

I'm so thankful for my life

There's always a lot of stuff going on in your head.

It is a machine that ticks along with an infinite amount of thoughts and reactions.

You're a great philosopher with a lot of thoughts now.

Maybe it's time to let go a bit or change the mindset.

Are you one of those people who always get an unexpected expense as soon as there is a penny to spare?

As soon as there has been some extra money, you expect that now there will be some unexpected cost, because it always does and what do you think it does then? After all, you get what you expect.

But it is also possible to change those habits of thinking to the fact that you constantly get unexpected income.

Start by being thankful that you actually had that extra money for the unexpected expense instead of cursing the expense.

Then when you feel and see that it is flowing, you continue to be grateful for every penny that is left.

And then you turn your thoughts and expectations to unexpected income instead.

What are my expectations?

I have positive expectations

You're in the flow now. The surprises are lined up and waiting for you.

Whatever it does that evokes that feeling you have now, make sure to keep it and happy surprises will keep knocking on your door.

When you are in the flow, everything is possible and things, events, people and circumstances pop up that take your breath away. It feels like you're living in another world almost.

But it's because you match the good energies that you get exactly what you want.

You have your focus set on the good things in life and expect the good things in life.

Just because you can't see something doesn't mean it doesn't exist. It is not there for you at the time because your focus is on something else so that the event passes you by.

But when you find the flow, no events that are in your dreams pass you by, but they match every time.

What are the events that affect me positively now?

I'm saving on glories

Now you have the control and balance back in your life.

You've found a middle ground that works for you.

Now things are moving much faster than before.

Sometimes it can feel like you're taking two steps forward and then three steps back.

It's your own limiting thoughts about yourself that make it so.

Dare to believe in yourself and your abilities. Sometimes it's a little hard to find what those limiting thoughts are, but when you hear yourself say Because after something, you get a hint of what it is.

For example, I can't get it, because..

It doesn't happen to me, because..

What you say after Because, is your limiting thoughts to work with.

What are my limiting thoughts?

I control my thoughts

Live in the here and now.

Life is not eternal.

Let go of the past and the future and embrace the present.

Don't wait until it's too late.

Constantly striving for something means that you don't live in the here and now.

Think about what you are striving for and why.

You struggle and struggle but never seem to get what you want anyway.

Then it's time for you to stop and fight now, stop interfering and trust that you will get what you are supposed to when it's time for it.

Also think about what it is you really need, what is it that you want?

Is it a nice new car, the latest clothes, mobiles and things and things?

Then it's your ego talking, because you're just as good without all the external things and you don't feel any better from them, maybe just for a little while.

But things come and go and when things disappear you stand there and feel bad again and have to start the hunt again.

You will never be satisfied.

What have I always had to fight for?

I let go and am satisfied

You are the hub of your life.

You receive everything you send out.

Now you're receiving a lot, but maybe not just what you want.

You are the one who decides what you want into your life. And you do that with what you focus on. What you focus on, you get in return, it's as simple as that.

So where is your focus?

Is it on the positive things that are in your life or is it the small negative elements?

Remember, the universe doesn't care if you want something or not. The universe only responds to and gives you more of what you are focused on.

That's why it's so important to be grateful for what you already have and focus on what you already have, that way you'll have more things to be thankful for in your life, whatever it is.

If you focus on what is not quite as you imagined, then you will get more of it.

Is your focus on the right things in your life?

I focus on all the positive things in my life

You want to learn something new.

Feels like a little challenge would be in place.

But you're hesitant about what others will think of what you want to learn.

Don't worry about what other people think about the things you want to do. If you want to learn Latin, you should learn Latin.

It's very important that you follow your heart and don't let other people's opinions affect you.

Be stubborn and don't give up.

Many writers, for example, have been rejected so many times that it is impossible to count, but have not given up, and have finally succeeded as well. Because they've had an inner conviction to fix it.

If you only have the belief that you can do it, you should do it, otherwise you betray yourself and tell yourself that you are not worthy of making your own decisions, but must always listen to what others say you can do.

No one knows better than you what you want and can do.

What would you like to learn in a new way?

I stand up for myself

You struggle and struggle to be heard and seen.

But at the same time, you want to be like everyone else, with the consequence that you and your unique abilities are invisible.

You have come into our universe with your special, unique gifts.

You've lived the life you have to learn certain things.

You are constantly trained with all the different encounters with people.

Everyone has something unique in them that we are meant to share with others.

But if you're constantly struggling to fit in and be like everyone else, you'll become one in the crowd and very anonymous.

Take advantage of and bring out the uniqueness about you, be proud that you are completely unique, think completely unique, look completely unique.

Imagine what a boring world it would be if everything looked exactly the same, all people, houses, animals, jobs, yes everything was exactly the same, it would be science fiction directly.

What special gifts do I have to share?

I'm proud of who I am

Don't be afraid of love.

Embrace love when it comes.

Dare to be vulnerable and be hit by the arrows of love.

Often you can see a pattern in your love relationships. What kind of love you are drawn to and above all what kind of love you think you are worthy.

Because that's what it's all about, what do you think you're worth in love?

For the universe knows that you are worthy of an infinite abundance of love, but can only respond to the vibrations you send out, anything else is impossible.

So what has your love life been like?

Dare to look at your relationships with objective eyes. How did you feel then, what were your thoughts, what were your expectations, etc

Only when you realize and consider yourself worthy of all good and all love can it come in its perfect form.

What has my love pattern been like?

I'm ready for new love

Take care of yourself and your health.

It's just as important as taking care of your inner self, don't forget that.

Balance is needed here too.

Just as important as it is to take care of your inner self, to work on yourself and your self-esteem.

It's just as important to take care of your body. This is the body you have been assigned in this life and that you will live in during your life's journey.

Then you have to take care of it, because you won't get anyone else.

It should take you steps towards your dream, it should guide you towards your dream, it should give you the power to take you towards your dream, it should nourish you to take you towards your dream.

If you mismanage your body, you won't be able to get around.

So make sure to give your body the sleep, food, and exercise it deserves.

What can I do for my body?

I'm afraid of me

You don't have to wander through the dark.

Lift your eyes and see all the clues you get.

Do not look backwards or forwards.

When you feel worried, anxious or sad about the future.

Keep in mind that these are just fantasies, you dream up a scenario that makes you feel the way you do.

That is not reality.

Because reality only exists now, tomorrow you don't know anything about.

How can I be more present?

I see where I am now

Now you've put yourself in a glass dome and are not receptive to the flow of your life.

You see a bright spot in the distance, but it can't reach you right now.

You stop the flow of your life if you can't receive. If you can't receive, you don't feel worthy.

What do you do when someone says something nice, gives you a compliment or wants to help you?

Do you thank and accept or do you just wave it away.

In order for the universe to deliver everything you desire, you must learn to receive EVERYTHING that is given to you and feel that you are worth it. Otherwise, stop the flow.

You should know that nothing is sent to you by chance and you need to receive it in order for you to be able to walk forward to everything you desire.

How can I act differently now?

I gratefully accept

Embark on a journey.

It's about a physical journey or a mental journey or both.

If you want to go on the journey of your dreams, you have to dare to dream big and be willing to do certain things.

If you don't reach the goal of your dreams, then you have to ask yourself: What am I not willing to do?

You have to be willing to do certain things to get going on your journey.

For example, if you want to move abroad, but are not willing to change your entire children's lives, yes, but then you will not get away either.

If you want to write a book, but don't contact a publisher, then it may not be a book.

You sometimes have to be willing to do certain things in order to get there and move forward.

What do I need to do to move forward?

I act in the direction of what I want

Think about what your thoughts are about the future.

Is it good or is it not so good.

You always have a choice in life.

It's always up to you to choose what you want.

We make many choices in life.

If someone insults you, you would most likely choose to take offense.

If someone gives you a compliment, you would choose to be happy.

But it's always a choice.

When you have to make a choice in life, anything, feel with your heart.

Ask the question and wait for the answer in the form of a feeling in your heart. You will clearly feel either a positive feeling about the right choice or an anxious feeling about the wrong choice.

Remember that whatever happens, what someone does or says, it's always your choice how you react to it.

How do I usually choose?

I make active choices

Lift your head and don't get bogged down in all the must-haves.

Sure, you have a lot of things to do all the time, but you can give it a new twist.

When we have a lot of things to do.

For example, to do laundry, shopping and shopping, you usually do it in the same order all the time, every time without thinking much about it. It's just a must-have to do.

Maybe you always start by doing laundry in the morning, then you clean and then go shopping. Everything is routine.

If, on the other hand, you first thing in the morning find out which of them would feel best to start with, you will end up in a better flow throughout the day.

You are in control and make an active choice.

When can I make active choices?

I control my flow

Make a deal with someone or yourself.

Make peace with someone or yourself.

Embrace the differences.

Let everyone be who they are. Try not to put labels on everything and everyone.

You can't control someone else's reality. You can't get things into other people's lives.

The only thing you can do is be true to yourself and let others be who they are.

You have to look after your own first, make sure you feel good.

Then you can also allow others to be who they are and not feel threatened by it. Then there will be ripples on the water and you spread what you have yourself to others.

Who do I need to accept as they are?

I like differences

Show who you are.

Dare to believe in your dream.

Believe in yourself and that you can do much more than you think.

What are you afraid of?

What's holding you back?

Why don't you take a chance?

What do you think could happen?

What you think might happen is only in your mind and you can change them. You are the only one who creates the obstacles.

Think of it this way:

Right now there are thousands of people on this earth who have done what I set out to do.

There are thousands who have made it.

I'm sure there are several people close to me who have managed it.

I'm not the first, others have.

Then your mental blocks are released, because you know it's not impossible.

What is my biggest fear right now?

I'm not alone

You are the superstar of your life.

You are on your way to creating the prosperity you want in your life.

Now it's your turn.

Prosperity is a mindset.

There are so many little things you can do to feel prosperity, to take you to prosperity.

Everyday luxury is what I'm talking about, pamper yourself a little.

Buy floral toilet paper instead of boring white.

Put on some bling bling, even if it's copies.

Set the table with fine porcelain for everyday use.

Spice up your outfit with a scarf for example.

Paint your nails.

Keep your car clean, tidy so it shines.

And so on, little things like this make you feel a little luxurious and attract prosperity and abundance.

What things do I need to polish up?

I'm luxurious

Let people you trust show you the way.

Take their advice to heart and follow it for a while.

This is how you can do it or maybe like this.

Surround yourself with people you look up to and trust. Read books, magazines about things you believe in. Listen to lectures by people you admire.

This will strengthen you greatly and soon people and events that you trust and admire will come to you for advice and guidance.

How can I give instead of how can I receive.

How can I help others instead of what can others give to me.

You've received and you're giving back.

Who or what inspires me?

I'm a role model

Believe in something.

Have faith that it works.

Embrace it instead of rejecting it outright.

The Law of Attraction works whether you believe it or not. So then you might as well learn the rules of the game, right?

Those who don't believe often say: What better way to keep thinking positive all the time? What's all that fluff?

Well, what better way to think negatively...

You send out energies all the time, whether you are aware of it or not.

Then it's better to know the rules instead of standing there in the middle of life and wondering why things turned out the way they did.

What do I believe in?

I'm embracing new ways of thinking

You are protected by a greater power.

There is always someone who looks out for your best interests.

Everyone in the universe is connected by their energies so you are never alone.

Feel safe.

You don't have to constantly walk around worrying about what you're thinking, that would be too hard.

You just need to pay attention to what you feel and ask yourself when you feel discomfort, what am I thinking?

It is your inner guidance system that warns that this is not you, now you are heading in the wrong direction.

Then you drop your attention to it and thank you for the information.

Don't resist the negative thoughts, because if you shout no to something, you draw attention to it and draw it into your life. Turn your thoughts away from the contrast and focus on what you want instead.

No, I don't want to be sick again like last year = discomfort

This year I'm so healthy and well, thank you =

contrast

Know that the universe will deliver more of what you want if only you turn your focus to it.

What does my focus look like?

I focus on what I want

You never stand still even if it feels like it.

You are constantly evolving.

You change the direction of your life.

Walking on new paths.

If you don't see the change in yourself, you feel like you're in the same place in your life.

Look at the people around you, look at what new acquaintances and events have come into your life.

Then you will see that you yourself have changed.

Otherwise, all this new stuff would never have come into your life.

Can I see the change in my life?

I'm constantly evolving

When things happen inside you, a lot happens outside of you as well.

Some people are left wondering what happened.

You yourself may be puzzled and wondering what happened.

Things happen all the time around us and we are influenced by everything. When you start working on yourself, it can easily become too much and it just becomes a mess of everything.

You think about everything and a little more and the law of attraction delivers more and more thoughts about those subjects.

You don't get ahead and get frustrated or confused.

You need to sort out all the topics and focus on one at a time. Feel free to write lists of the topics because then it is even easier to sort.

The Law of Attraction will still deliver lots of thoughts, but now it's on the same topic and you're keeping up.

How can I divide my life into slices of cake?

I'm moving forward

You have the power to break free, you don't have to be trapped behind an invisible wall.

You have all the protection and guidance you need as long as you dare to trust that everything will work out.

How come you believe in all the fears, that bad things will happen.

It is you who paints it in your mind.

Then you can well believe in your dreams that you paint as well.

What is it that makes you believe in one but not the other?

Aren't you worth it? Well you are worth it all.

Has it never happened before? Sometime should be the first. And there you have a hint as to why it hasn't happened, you don't think it's going to happen and here you go is the universe.

What fears do I usually portray?

I believe in my dreams

Look how beautiful you are.

See what beauty is in you.

Spread your wings and believe in yourself.

You are counted here in the universe,. You are needed to maintain balance, otherwise you wouldn't be here right now. You are in the right place and time. The universe makes no mistakes.

Nothing is a coincidence.

You support others by being you. By being yourself and not like everyone else. By being a strong and clear role model. By being healthy, believing in yourself, you stimulate others to have the same desire.

When you allow yourself to be you even though others don't like it, you encourage others to do so.

Be yourself.

What makes me different from everyone else?

I like me

You have a tendency to take away something of yourself.

You give up parts of your dreams because others don't believe in it.

You think you know what you want, but give up if it doesn't happen.

Many times we think we know exactly what we want.

Always trust that the universe knows what's best for you and sends it your way.

Was it a particular house you wanted, a special relationship, or a job, but you didn't get it.

Then the universe is telling you that it wasn't good enough for you and that something much better is on the way. Something that will suit you perfectly.

So be happy and excited about what's to come.

What is it that has happened around me when I have lost a dream?

I'm excited

Time to welcome some new things, events, and people into your life.

If you think that your life looks the same all the time, it's probably because you're so focused on reality, what is, and can't see any other scenario.

And then the change comes very slowly or not all and the essence of your life looks very similar.

But in order for you to make a change, you have to start using your imagination a little more. Ignore what you are observing, what is right now, and what people around you are observing.

And start focusing and dreaming about how you would like it to be instead, what you would like your life to look like.

Only then can there be a change in your life.

The Law of Attraction kicks in immediately and gives you more thoughts and experiences about what you focus on wanting.

What new things can I choose in my life?

I can change my life

Remember that no one can take over your life.

Only you are in control of it and invite you to experience what you want to experience.

Stay in control.

Even if the universe gives you what you focus on, you may need to do things actively. You can't just sit on your butt and wait for things to land in your lap or for opportunities to knock on your door, although it's not impossible.

Of course, you should hand over control to the universe and trust delivery, but you have to act on impulses, etc.

You can't just throw a lump of clay on a potter's wheel and think it's going to shape. You have to work with it and help shape it the way you want it.

Can I do something active today?

I'm in control

You have a great power in you.

Feel that you are like God, who can give everything, fulfill everything for yourself and others.

You are pure vibrating energy. Everything in the entire universe is pure vibrating energy.

If you look at solid matter under a microscope, you would see a vibrating energy mass. All energy vibrates at a certain frequency. You, too, vibrate at a certain frequency because you are also energy. And what frequency you vibrate at is up to you with your thoughts and feelings.

So that's why it's so important that you feel good in order to send out good frequency and attract things and events that vibrate with the same frequency.

You cannot listen to p4 if you have set the frequency to p3.

What can I do to feel good today?

I choose joy

Your greatest security lies with your family.

There you can be just as you are.

Giving and receiving unconditional love.

    Keep in mind that family doesn't have to be related by blood. You may have other people around you who are at least as important as a family and sometimes even more important.

    You can always find security and joy in these people, they are your fixed point in life.

    You get and feel so much joy with them.

    Imagine sitting and watching your peaceful, sleeping child, there is no greater love and security.

    You meet a friend and just get happy and your whole body.

    What does my family look like?

    I give joy

You feel almost invincible now.

You get exuberant ideas all the time that lead you forward.

When you get into a flow like this and feel as good as you do now, now is the time to take care of a lot of things and make decisions, because then it will be right.

Avoid making decisions when you don't have flow and positive thoughts.

Now you have to keep believing in yourself and not let the ego come in and control you, because then you will stagnate.

The ego is only there to get in your way, the ego just wants to be liked by everyone else, it's your social mask and is constantly afraid of not being good enough.

The ego is not your true self, who you are deep down, you know you can.

How can I disregard my ego?

I'm true to myself

Someone needs you now.

A close friend, colleague or loved one is not feeling as well as they could.

You can never change someone else's reality. They can only do that with their own thoughts.

What you can do is lead by example, let them be in your joy, send them loving thoughts, see for yourself solutions to their problems.

Redirect conversations to positive things and feel as good as you can yourself to infect the other person.

You always feel better in the energy of other loving people.

If you feel good and you have people close to you who feel bad, it's because you want to help and learn something.

If you feel bad and you have people close to you who feel bad, then you have attracted it because of how you feel and then you know that it is time to change your mindset.

How can I influence others today?

I spread love

You read and study a lot now.

You devour information and take lots of courses.

You close in on yourself.

In your pursuit of happiness, it is very easy for you to go overboard.

Remember, you have a lot of information inside you already. You need to let it sink in and treat it as well and not just refill all the time.

Use the information constructively.

Like you refill a glass of water and never stop beating, it just overflows and goes to waste. You need to drink the water as well and let your body and mind absorb it in order to refill it.

What do I need to let go of to let it come to me?

I can

You're stuck in the same place because you have such a hard time choosing.

Weigh the pros and cons.

All the time in our lives, we are faced with choices. Then you can feel with intuition as I mentioned earlier.

But you can also think about where you stand in life.

If you are satisfied, you do not need to start thinking anew and you can calmly walk on the safe path, then you know what you have and get.

But if you feel that it's time for a change, you need to challenge yourself a bit by choosing the more uncertain path, where you don't have a given outcome and must have faith that everything will work out for the best.

What do you choose?

Do I have a choice to make?

I trust my gut

Playfulness dominates you now.

You feel in love. In love with life. In love with yourself. In love with friends. In love with the family.

True happiness is unparalleled.

True happiness does not depend on circumstances being a certain way.

True Happiness does not say:

If you get rid of that, get that stuff and get that in order... Then I show up.

Happiness is within you.

How can I feel happiness within?

I'm allowed to be happy

You're searching for treasures.

You're looking for happiness in the wrong places.

You don't have to put in that much effort.

In today's society with the rush to the GREAT happiness, we are constantly fed with information and we have to outdo each other with cooler and cooler experiences and things to find the GREAT happiness.

Then it's easy to forget the lasting real happiness that is there all the time, namely everyday happiness.

The happiness of seeing your child curiously wake up to a new day, the happiness that the sun is shining, the happiness over flowered toilet paper instead of white, the happiness of a nice bouquet of flowers, the happiness of the sun peeking out, the happiness when your pet lovingly plays, the happiness of a cup of coffee, etc

Where is my everyday happiness?

I'm curious about life

You're having a bit of a turmoil in some areas of your life.

There are fears and insecurities behind it.

Work with them and let them go and you will arrive and climb up.

When you want to change your thoughts about something, you can't go from 0-100 at once, because then you don't believe in yourself and then it becomes backwards.

You have to convince yourself slowly but surely, change your values and thoughts so you can believe in it step by step. So your psyche is keeping up.

If we take money for example:

Short of money, never enough.

But if I start planning a little better, maybe think twice before I buy something, then it will last a little longer.

The money lasts a little longer now and that means that I will soon be able to put aside a few cents for what I want.

I can actually control how much I spend.

I am on my way to financial balance.

What thoughts can I begin to change?

I can change my life

Try to get balance in your life.

Try to focus on one thing at a time and put your faith in it.

Having too many things in the air at the same time erodes the power within you.

It is not possible to hope for a positive result while sending out negative signals.

For example, if you've applied for a job, but then think you're probably not going to get it.

Then there's no point in applying for it at all.

Even if you want to protect yourself from disappointment, you can't sit on two chairs at the same time.

You may not be able to prevent negative thoughts, but you can pay attention to them and correct them. Believe that it will work out in the best way by saying, for example: Don't know yet how, but it will work out.

In what situations do I need to be more positive?

Everything works out in the best way

You see the strengths, power, and personality of others.

You lift others up and can rejoice with others.

This will allow you to bring it to you yourself.

It serves you nothing to be jealous of other people's successes and gains.

Jealousy only attracts more circumstances and events to be jealous of.

Do all you can to rejoice with others, feel their happiness, and be inspired.

Because when someone close to you gets what you wanted, it means that it's on its way to you too. The universe is showing the way and you are matching your energy to it. Otherwise, you would never have gotten a taste of what it can be like through them, you would never have seen it up close.

Continue to trust and be happy for them and it will come to you as well.

What successes are there in my vicinity to be happy about?

I'm inspired

When others go to the right, go to the left.

When others want to get ahead, you stand completely still.

No matter how many people say Yes, you can say No.

The more true you can be to yourself, the better you'll feel.

If you know that something is right for you, then it is so regardless of what others think, say and do.

The more you practice this, the better it gets.

You can't afford to ignore yourself, you have to demand that respect for yourself.

Be like the against the grain and lovingly question why someone thinks this or that about something.

It's not about convincing others of your point of view, it's about showing that you should believe in yourself and dare to stand up for who you are and follow your dreams.

How can I listen more to myself?

I'm responsive

You hesitate, have no real faith. Why?

That faith can move mountains is absolutely true.

If you don't have the faith that you will get what you want, it doesn't matter how much you want something.

It doesn't matter that you want it with every fiber in your body, if you don't think it's possible, so be it.

I want 100000 SEK now, but deep down I don't think it's possible now, even though I can feel how wonderful it would be. Then, of course, you don't get 100000 SEK.

You have to find the feeling within you where you believe it is actually possible, that feeling is personal.

There may be those who really feel that it is possible to get 100000 just like that, but you may believe that you can get 50 SEK, then you start there.

Where do I draw the line for what I can believe in?

I believe in my feelings

What can you believe in.

You don't really know what is fantasy or reality.

You both believe and you don't.

You don't need to know what is dream and what is reality. You just need to trust and go with it.

Sometimes there are so many things going on and you want to have an explanation for everything and you rationalize it away luckily or something.

You see things happen, but you still don't think you're in control of everything with your thoughts and feelings. You wish for something and it happens, but you still find it hard to believe it's you.

How much proof do you need?

I had a dream that I was a butterfly, I woke up and a thought struck me, what do I know.

Am I a human being who dreams that I am a butterfly or am I a butterfly who dreams that I am a human being?

Let the boundaries be erased.

What are the small miracles I have in my life?

I love that I'm in charge

What am I worth.

Do I have any value at all.

It's all about the eyes you see with.

You deserve everything you get in life. Everything that comes your way and everything you experience, you have earned.

Then some people think, oh well, I'm not better than this "life" I have. Everything has gone against me, but then I'm no better worth it. And so the "life" continues.

Or you look at it that because I've had the life I have with quite a lot of adversity, I deserve everything from here and now.

I deserve to get everything I desire.

I deserve to be peaceful.

I deserve to feel satisfied.

I deserve to feel good.

I deserve all the best.

I deserve to love me.

How has my life been?

I deserve everything I want

Might be good to actually gather your thoughts.

It will be easier to know where to go if you have smaller pieces to focus on.

If you get too scattered in your thoughts, you will get scattered results.

The universe will have a bit of a hard time delivering what you want if you're unclear.

If you focus on both blue and yellow at the same time, it will be green. And that's not really what you wanted, even though the ingredients are there.

So it pays to focus on one color at a time, because then the universe has a chance to give you exactly what you want and it goes much straighter and faster.

What part do I need to focus on?

I know what I want

Now it's time to be a little more playful.

Don't take life so seriously.

Relax and have some fun too.

Remember to have fun in life too. Life shouldn't just consist of a lot of must-haves.

You only have one life.

Try to always have something you think is fun planned in the calendar.

Then you'll always have something to look forward to. You'll be happier and feel better.

Plan a day to pamper yourself, a little weekend trip, a dance night, a course or whatever else you think is fun.

Be sure to book it in as well and not just think that you want to do it.

Everything will be so much easier with a fun activity booked, because the universe will deliver more fun then.

Do I have any fun things planned?

I choose to have fun

Congratulations you have now made it through what you consider trouble.

It brightens up for you and you step out of this as a much stronger person.

We go through life and make a lot of mistakes and that's what we're going to do. We will learn from it and move forward with new insights.

So give thanks and accept when you make a mistake, because then you have developed a lot and can find new ways.

It's when you completely give up that it becomes a failure, you don't even try to see new paths or have made enough mistakes. You realize that this is not your path, but you should make a lot of mistakes first, it's so healthy and natural.

It's all about how you look at things.

What mistakes have I made that I can re-evaluate?

I receive development

Dare to change direction.

Dare to let go of the old to walk new paths.

When you get a sign of a new way to go, take the chance.

Take the chance and trust that it will be right. The universe doesn't give you new paths without having a meaning to it. Even if you don't see the point of it right now, it will show up later on, trust it.

You might suddenly be fired from your job. Don't despair over it, but trust that something new and exciting is on the horizon.

A new job may be coming into your life that will suit you perfectly, and if you hadn't been fired, the new job wouldn't have been able to come to you. Maybe you're going to inherit a lot of money and don't need to work anymore. You may need to move to meet the love of your life.

The possibilities are endless as long as you trust that everything that happens has a cause and meaning.

What new paths are there for me?

I'm looking for opportunities

Don't hesitate.

You know deep down what you want, have the confidence to believe in it.

Nothing is too big, stupid or weird.

You can do anything you want.

Don't be discouraged by people who stop your dreams. Don't be discouraged by people who think a lot of things about your dreams. Don't be discouraged by negative people telling you all the problems of your dreams.

Choose carefully who you tell your dreams to, choose people who will give you support and backup for your dreams.

Especially in the beginning, so as not to absorb their possible negative comments.

Have the courage to always follow your dreams. And others will follow you.

Do I have the courage to follow my dreams?

I'm brave

You are a warm person who likes to lift others.

You help and support all the time.

A big part of you wants to help everyone. You are so caring and wish everyone well.

So sometimes in your quest to help, you can easily forget about those closest to you. It's not meant that way and nothing conscious from you, it just happens that way.

And you are also part of your closest circle. Remember that you have to help yourself as well, otherwise you don't consider yourself important enough. And then you're likely to just be taken advantage of by others.

Give yourself the same advice and help that you give others, put yourself first. And it's absolutely nothing selfish, but it's necessary for you to have something to help others with.

Give yourself the tools and guidance you need to give others.

What advice can I give myself?

I'm my best friend

There are ulterior motives to everything.

Don't trust anyone.

Everyone wants something.

Or?

You have to learn to trust people. If you go around distrusting people, the universe will only deliver you such people.

You need to start trusting people and what they say. Realize that it has nothing to do with you if they don't keep their promises, it says more about that person themselves. That person considers themselves superior to everyone else and doesn't have to care about other people's feelings.

First, start trusting yourself, stand by what you say and do, and people around you will respect you and not be deceived.

Just because one person is deceived doesn't mean everyone has to, believe good of everyone in the first place. Don't lug on past experiences.

What are my thoughts about others?

I can trust people

You feel so free and beautiful.

Beauty comes from within.

You start to feel worthy of everything and have a good self-esteem.

The most attractive thing there is is people who don't have the need to put others down in order to lift themselves. People who stand firmly on the ground and have a good self-esteem.

Are confident in who they are and lift others to feel the same. Lift others up and rather stand back yourself to give others the praise, because you don't need to be acknowledged all the time. It doesn't matter to you.

Don't care what others think about the things they do, but believe in themselves.

It brings such joy to see others grow and believe in yourself.

You see that you are worth everything without others having to sacrifice anything, that everyone can partake of the infinite source of the universe without having to put anyone else down.

Who can I lift today?

I can praise others

Want to build a nest.

Take care of and appreciate what you have.

Take care of everything around you.

To attract the right things, you have to appreciate what you already have.

If you are careless with what you have and don't give a damn about it, you can never attract better things.

If you don't care about and appreciate the relationships you have in your life right now, you can't attract anything better.

The universe always matches the feelings you have.

Take two car owners, one takes care of, keeps clean and appreciates his car and the other lets his car be dirty and messy.

Which one do you think attracts even better cars?

What can I be more careful about?

I appreciate my stuff

The answer is right in front of you.

Think outside the box to see.

Stop looking and hunting and you will see more clearly.

Is it possible that there are angels who are with you?

Is it possible that I can get everything I put my focus on?

Is it possible that there is a greater force working for me and helping me move forward in life?

Is it possible that there are a lot of things that are invisible to me around me?

Is it possible that I can get what I want?

Is it possible that we are all connected in a common energy field?

Is it possible that I have personal guides?

Yes, anything is possible, as long as you can open up a little more and let go of your old values and think a little outside the box.

What is it in you that says it couldn't be possible?

How can I think in new ways?

Anything Really Is Possible

You read and study a lot.

But what is it that you really want?

What is your intention?

You can't just go on and study, read without having a goal with it.

You must have an intention with your studies or they will not do you any good.

Because it's not the reading itself that takes you anywhere, it's how you manage what you read that gives you a change.

Sure, you can learn a lot of things and store them in your brain, but what's the use of that if you don't have a purpose for your study.

You have to be able to do something active with what you're learning, otherwise it's just a waste of time.

Always be the energy you intend to attract with your studies.

What am I reading right now?

I'm in a state of change

Time to regain control of your life.

You're a bit of an outsider right now.

You're in, but you're not.

Every time you think you have the right to be upset because of how someone treated you. When you feel you have the right to be angry, hurt or sad.

Then you have handed over your control of your well-being to others to do what you want with.

Then you feel left out of yourself, you don't have control and make yourself a victim.

It is never, ever possible to hand over the responsibility to someone else, because it is always your thoughts that evoke your feelings.

Do I see situations where I've handed over control?

I am my responsibility

Don't undervalue yourself.

Believe that you are your own creator.

It may be difficult to see and believe that you create all the experiences in your own life.

Start looking around and see when the law of attraction is at work in other people's lives, then it will be more visible.

You will see that those who talk about wealth, are.

Those who say they feel good, do it.

Those who talk about diseases, have it.

Those who say they have no money are poor.

Then you can start to see that it applies to you as well.

If you feel lonely, you will be.

If you feel poor, you will be.

If you feel rich, you will be.

What you feel, you are more attracted to, and there is no one who is exempt from this natural law.

What am I talking about?

I feel what I want

A change in you is coming.

You've discovered that parts of you can be hidden with a change of thought.

All your thoughts you've been thinking all your life are still in you. Everything you've ever felt remains in you.

You can't delete past thoughts.

However, not all thoughts are active at the moment and therefore hidden from you.

So you can't change a thought or perception because it's a part of you, but you can choose a different thought and perception.

You can't take away one thought, but you can activate the next one that feels better and you will attract matching thoughts that make the thought you don't want not become dominant, but is put very far back and loses strength.

What thoughts do I want to weaken?

I choose good thoughts

You've come a long way in your development now.

But you still have a hard time trusting yourself.

Red or green light. Angel or devil on your shoulder. Calm or uneasiness in the stomach.

Always trust what your intuition tells you. If you have resistance in you to do something, don't do it. It's not the right time for that, and it won't turn out the way you thought it would.

Everything has a meaning even if you don't see it right away, but always trust your feelings.

If it's a red light, listen to it. If it's a green light, listen to it.

If you have a hard time finding your feeling, take a moment and think about different events in your life.

What was your feeling, how did you do it and what was the result? Then you can guess what your feeling is.

I was going out to a party once and had been looking forward to it, but at the same time there was a little resistance in me. The party was canceled, I felt a little disappointed but at the same time I was sure that it had a meaning that would show itself. At night, I got out on assignments that I wouldn't have been able to if I had been out at a party myself. So it had a meaning.

How can I practice my intuition?

*I listen to my gut *

Make some plans for the future.

Set clear goals.

Make visual goals that you can see every day.

You've probably heard that you make a Vision Board to clarify your dreams in a collage.

What many people do is to cut out pictures of what they want and also write texts for. You stick it on a board and hang it up so you can see it every day.

But what many people forget is the feeling.

Sure, I see a picture of a nice house, a nice car and maybe a lot of money, but what kind of feelings do they give you?

Are you happy, are you excited, do you feel good when you see the pictures or do you feel that you don't know how this is going to happen, they have the nice car but not me, I can't get that much money.

Try to figure out how you want to feel first, then look for images that are connected to the feeling.

If you want to be happy, maybe a picture of the world's cutest kitten will give you that feeling, even though you may not want and want a cat.

If you want to feel freedom, maybe a picture of a beautiful landscape from Austria will give you that feeling instead of a picture of money.

What is it that I really want to feel in my life?

I have goals in my life

Open your eyes to alternative routes.

There is never just one way that is right.

A thing never just looks a certain way, but has lots of shapes.

If someone says chair to you, you will automatically get your picture of a chair.

But just because your chair, in your mind, looks like that, doesn't mean everyone else does.

They are available in lots of models, colors, sizes and shapes.

So it is with your desires as well.

If you see a path to your desires, the universe has many more models, colors, sizes and shapes on them.

So don't lock yourself into your ways, because then the universe will have a hard time giving you opportunities because the universe has to respond to your vibration according to the law of attraction.

How can I see more roads?

I wish and let go

Are you prepared to have your dreams.

Are you prepared for it to go fast now.

Don't worry, you won't get more than you're ready for.

Sometimes things go fast towards our dreams. It almost feels unreal how much flow you have. Is this really happening to me, are questions that come up.

You always get what you can handle, trust it.

It may seem that if you get everything you want, you wouldn't be scared, but it can actually happen. Usually it's because you're so afraid of losing it again or you don't think you're worth it after all.

But that's why there's a kind of delay in the universe as well. So that you have time to get used to it and sort out what you really want.

Because it would be a bit strange if you thought of an elephant and bang it was there in the living room.

You always have a chance to think and feel what you want and when you're ready, it comes. When you feel it with your whole being that it can be so, that you are worth it and that you just relax and receive what comes.

Am I ready?

I'm ready

Research something.

Seek information about what's on your mind.

It will lead you further.

If you have questions about something that you might wish for, it may be a good idea to search for some information about it.

Talking all the time about letting go of how, where and when to the universe to figure out.

But if you are a curious person, it can be very difficult to completely let go. Then it can help to investigate, do some research on the subject and thus reassure yourself that there are lots of ways to achieve what you want.

For example, if you want to be a writer, but don't know how to do it, it can stop you because you think too much about the How, which is not your job to know.

Search for some information about how others have done it, what opportunities there are, what courses there are, what kind of books there are, etc.

Then you calm yourself by seeing that there really are so many paths to become a writer and that lots of other people have done it before.

And then it can be easier to let go of How to the universe.

Where do I need to do some research?

All roads lead to Rome

Förlag: BoD – Books on Demand, Stockholm, Sverige
Tryck: BoD – Books on Demand, Norderstedt, Tyskland
ISBN: 978-91-8057-481-5